Arc WYMOI in WORLD WAR TWO

Philip Yaxley

JOHN NICKALLS PUBLICATIONS

Published by

John Nickalls Publications

Oak Farm Bungalow, Sawyers Lane, Suton, Wymondham, Norfolk, NR18 9SH.

First impression : November 2010

© Philip Yaxley

ISBN 978 1904136 31 6

Design and typesetting :
Tim Smith www.spacepenguin.co.uk

Frontispiece Photo:
Briton Brush Company fire-watchers A.J. "Bunty" Long
and George Mabbutt at their post.

Contents

Hitler will send no warning – so always carry your gas mask

ISSUED BY THE MINISTRY OF HOME SECURITY

Acknowledgements

I wish to record my special thanks to the ladies of Archant's library, together with Janet Smith and Mary Garner of the Wymondham Town Archive, all of whom have been most helpful.

I am indebted to the following for permission to use photographs: Archant, Joan Allen, John Ayton, Arthur Banham, Eric Barnicoat, Richard Bartram, Paul Bevis, Tony Bradstreet, the late Joan Bunn, Fred Bushell, Philip Chapman, Edith Childerhouse, Jean Clarke, Jill Clarke, Alan Coombe, Joy Easton, Milton Edelman, the late Richard Fryer, Ron Green, Ann Hoare, Fred Hoftgartner, Martin Jeffery, Bob Lister, the late George Mabbutt, Pat Ramm, Tim Semmence, Peggy Sheldrake, the late Clifford Temple, Roy West, Wymondham Town Archive and the 389th Bomb Group Memorial Museum at Hethel (Fred Squires).

I have endeavoured to trace all copyright holders and if I have not contacted anyone please accept my apologies.

Many people have offered snippets of information, but in particular I would like to mention Beryl Brown, Gerald Button, George Gosling, Ann Hoare, Barry Plunkett, Colin Proctor, Fred Squires, Peter Wharton and Browick Road School (Darryl Long).

Special thanks to Terry Burchell for his photographic work, Caroline Hogan for typing duties and John Nickalls, the publisher.

In 1940 Joe Smith's garage in White Horse Street (see page 24) was offering new bicycles for sale. With petrol rationed and restrictions on its use bicycles became a popular means of getting about during the war.

Wymondham in the late 1930s

In the late 1930s Wymondham was a lively market town of some 5,100 inhabitants and had seen progress on many fronts. The laying of a water and sewerage system in 1932-33 and the opening of a Senior School (now part of the High School) off Norwich Road in May 1939 were just two major projects which would benefit townsfolk. Significantly in March 1935 the parish council had been elevated to urban district status with a greater control over its own affairs.

Wymondham's Market Street presented a tranquil, even sleepy, appearance on a hot May Sunday in 1937.

Seen here decorated for the 1937 Coronation, the Norwich Corporation Electricity Department's showroom had been opened at Caius House in Middleton Street in 1933.

Mr William R Purchase, headmaster of the Browick Road Central Boys School, is seen here with pupils working on the school magazine in 1934. Among the boys are Arthur Banham (first left sitting), who was to serve with the R.A.F. in India, and Alan Hammond (centre sitting), who joined the Fire Brigade. On 14 May 1940 Mr Purchase, who had become headmaster of the town's new Senior School a year earlier, was the first Wymondham man to enrol in War Minister Anthony Eden's Local Defence Volunteers (L.D.V.'s) – and 300 local men followed him the same day! The busy headmaster would also be instrumental in organizing 'Dig for Victory' lectures and the formation of a branch of the Air Training Corps.

The Regal Cinema opened in March 1937 and would prove to be a real morale-booster during the war.

The machine room of the Briton Brush Company's factory in Lady's Lane and the staff of the Wymondham Laundry, situated on Norwich Road, both pictured just before the war. These concerns and others, like the Co-operative Wholesale Society's brush works at Chapel Lane, provided much employment in the locality and were to lose many valued workers to the fight against Hitler.

1938-1939

30 September 1938 – *Prime Minister Neville Chamberlain returned from meeting Hitler in Munich and declared 'Peace in our time'.*

1 September 1939 – *Germany invaded Poland.*

3 September 1939 – *Britain and France declared war on Germany and British Expeditionary Force began to leave for France.*

17 December 1939 – *The German pocket-battleship Graf Spee was scuttled by her crew on the River Plate in Uruguay.*

Although Wymondham may have presented a calm appearance as storm clouds were gathering over Europe, local preparations for an inevitable war were being put in hand.

WYMONDHAM URBAN COUNCIL OFFICES, MIDDLETON STREET

The offices of Wymondham Urban District Council are pictured soon after they were opened by Sir Bartle Frere, vice-chairman of Norfolk County Council, on 28 March 1938. It would fall to the Urban District Council, first under the chairmanship of Harry Clarke then for most of the war Edwin Gooch, to coordinate Wymondham's response to the threat of enemy attack. The council would depend on a whole army of volunteers, of which fire-watchers, air raid wardens, home guard members and evacuee helpers were just some. The Women's Voluntary Service (WVS) undertook many duties from fund-raising and knitting comforts for the troops to helping evacuees and driving ambulances. All the volunteers would have appreciated the slogan 'Civil defence is common sense'.

Council Offices,
WYMONDHAM.

Dear Sir/Madam,
The Fire Guard Plan & Fire Guard Training.

The early introduction of the Fire Guard Plan in Wymondham calls for the speeding up of training of Fire Guards. The responsibility of reporting and dealing with fires caused by enemy action during the night will be transferred to the Fire Guard Organisation and to ensure the effectiveness of the Plan suitable training must be given.

Under the new Fire Guard Orders all Fire Guards are required to undertake this training and arrangements have been made for instruction to be given at...
COUNCIL OFFICES WEDNESDAY JANUARY 5.
7:0 P M.

Will you please attend this Meeting and bring with you any adult members of your household who may be interested. It is realised that the majority of people in Wymondham would be ready and willing to help the Fire Guards in the event of enemy action but a knowledge of the Fire Guard Plan and of the correct manner in which to tackle incendiary bombs and resultant fires would considerably increase their usefulness.

Yours faithfully
J. H. PRIOR.
Fire Guard Officer

The recruiting of fire guards was already underway when this notice was issued in early January 1938. Lieutenant Colonel J.H.Prior, who lived at The Priory in Middleton Street and was a Boer War veteran, was appointed Fire Guard officer. Later he became Commanding Officer of the Wymondham Local Defence Volunteers and then for a time the local Home Guard.

WYMONDHAM URBAN DISTRICT COUNCIL
GAS MASKS

Gas Masks will be issued on Friday (Sept. 30th) 5 p.m. - 10 p.m. at

The SCHOOLS SPOONER ROW

You must call personally so that you may be given the correct size

Instructions for use will be given to you when you receive the Mask

27th September, 1938   L. STANDLEY
                                    Clerk

In late September 1938 the town's bellman announced that gas masks would be distributed from the Fairland Hall, while Spooner Row folk collected theirs from the village school. Babies up to two years old were provided with respirator bags, while young children loved their Mickey Mouse gas masks.

AIR RAID PRECAUTIONS
(CASUALTY SERVICES)

Volunteers (Male and Female) urgently required for the above Section of Wymondham's Air Raid Precautions Scheme. Will Ladies or Gentlemen who wish to join please send their names, or apply for forms to:

M. C. AYTON,
A.R.P. OFFICER,
Council Offices,
Wymondham

FIRST AID LECTURES which are FREE will commence on January 3rd, 1939

From May 1938 the Air Raid Precautions (ARP) Committee met once a month and it was reported in December that 40 wardens were in training. However, in early January 1939 Captain Malcolm Ayton, the ARP officer, was still appealing for more volunteers.

Through 1939 and long after hostilities commenced volunteers were always needed for essential duties.

WYMONDHAM URBAN DISTRICT COUNCIL.

AIR RAID PRECAUTIONS.

Air Raid Wardens,
First Aid and Medical Services,
Rescue and Demolition Services,
Decontamination Service, and
Dispatch Rider Sections.

Enrolment of Volunteers

URGENT AND IMPORTANT.

The Local Authority in response to Urgent Communications from the Secretary of State for the Home Department, based on the highest advice in the National Interest, are now organising the following Air Raid Precautions Services:—

(a) Air Raid Wardens.
(b) First Aid and Medical Services.
(c) Rescue and Demolition Services.
(d) Decontamination of Materials Service.
(e) Dispatch Riders.

The Local Authority therefore invite Applications from members of the Public who are able and willing to serve as Volunteers in connection with any of the above Services, and they earnestly trust that there will be a large and immediate response to this Appeal, which is made in the interests of the Community and of the Nation at large.

The Secretary of State has instituted a Badge for distribution to persons who volunteer for Air Raid Precautions Services and who undergo the necessary training. With the approval of His Majesty the King, the Royal Crown will be incorporated with the Badge.

Form of Application for Enrolment as an Air Raid Warden, or Form of Application for Enrolment in the First Aid or Medical Service, Rescue Parties, Decontamination Squads or Dispatch Rider sections, with brief particulars of the duties to be performed, may be obtained at the undermentioned Offices:

WYMONDHAM URBAN DISTRICT COUNCIL,
COUNCIL OFFICES,
WYMONDHAM.

NOTE:—Men who have any reserve obligations to the Navy, Army or Air Force, or to a Police Force or Fire Brigade, or who are enrolled as Special Constables should not apply for enrolment in the Air Raid Precautions Organisation.

Copyright Form A.R.15. SHAW & SONS LTD., Fetter Lane, E.C.4. E 57766-8

The Vicarage Room in Church Street where women were trained in first aid and home nursing. In July 1938 32 women successfully completed a course in ARP and first aid duties. Early in the war the building was used as a social centre for evacuee mothers four afternoons a week, the sessions being run by the WVS and tea provided for 1d (less than 1p) a cup. The military also used the building and dances were held there. The Abbey Hall now stands on the site.

One of the greatest protections against the dangers of air attack after nightfall was the blackout. All street lighting was extinguished, houses were forbidden to show light which was visible from the outside and vehicle headlights had to be screened. Blackout practices were held in July and August 1939, while it was reported on 1 September that many folk were buying dark material and paper as a total blackout had been ordered from that day. During the war several Wymondham people were fined by the local magistrates' court for infringements of the blackout rules.

Captain Malcolm Ayton is pictured in his uniform whilst serving in the 9th Battalion of the Home Guard. He had been Wymondham's organizer-instructor of the town's ARP services for over 14 months when war broke out on Sunday 3 September 1939. A few days before he had been asked by a reporter whether the town was prepared for an emergency and he replied: "Yes, Wymondham is ready". But in the event there was still much that needed to be done.

A family air raid shelter in a garden of a house on the Lizard. Anderson shelters, which were made of corrugated iron and were dropped about three feet in the ground then covered with earth, were distributed from September 1939. Later Morrison shelters, constructed in the form of a metal table with detachable wire-mesh sides, were issued to other residents for use indoors. Eventually in the town 216 homes had Anderson shelters and 285 had Morrisons. Ten big public trench shelters had been excavated at various points, including ones on the Fairland, the King's Head Meadow and the Browick Road recreation ground. By mid-October 1939 'To The Trenches' notices had appeared around the town. Each shelter could accommodate up to thirty people and they were intended 'to be useful to those caught in an air raid' who were away from home or work.

Sandbags protecting the Police Station, then situated at the Bridewell, soon after the outbreak of war. District Superintendent S.H.Bushell is on the left. Sandbag revetments were also built at strategic points around the town, while a siren was mounted on a telegraph pole at the police station. It made a warbling sound for a warning of air attack and a steady note for the all-clear. In 1939, during what was termed 'The Phoney War', Wymondham only experienced three air raid warnings.

A decontamination centre was established in this unobtrusive building in Back Lane in late 1939. There was also a mortuary in the same street, which from 1941 had an overflow unit at the Tithe Barn near the King's Head Meadow. The building, whose top can be seen in the background, was used by the military.

Brenda Smith (later Lincoln), secretary to Mr Swann at the Norwich Corporation Electricity Department's shop, was one of many many volunteers who came forward for a whole range of vital duties. She is seen here practising a decontamination procedure in pits off Norwich Road.

Members of the Wymondham Auxiliary Fire Service at the beginning of the war. Charlie Saul is in the centre of the front row and George Chapman, who also became the town's evacuee billeting officer, is second left in the back row. The brigade were to play a key role on the local home front, particularly dealing with incidents resulting from the many incendiary bombs that fell and assisting during the Norwich blitz.

The fire station in Market Street, the second building on the left with a lamp protruding from the front, was a hive of activity. In 1939 one fireman had to sleep there each night.

By November 1939 the many forces personnel stationed in the neighbourhood could avail themselves of the recreational and refreshment facilities at the Ex-Servicemen's Club in Queen Street (left hand picture), the Men's Club in Market Street (partially seen on the immediate left in the right hand picture), the Masonic Hall in Damgate and the Methodist schoolroom in Town Green. Troops were encamped at Kimberley Park, Dykebeck Farm, Silfield and Wicklewood, while a number of buildings around the town, including the Fairland Hall, were requisitioned for military accommodation. The ARP wardens went out on night patrols from the guardroom in the Men's Club.

On 4 September 1939 972 evacuee children, together with some mothers, helpers and teachers, arrived in Wymondham by bus from Great Yarmouth where they had disembarked from two pleasure steamers the Royal Daffodil and the Golden Eagle. The boats had brought them from Gravesend the previous day. The picture shows a party of evacuee children being escorted from the Senior School, which acted as a reception centre, to their new homes around the town. An evacuee sub-committee, including the Women's Voluntary Service, helped with their dispersal. Overseeing the distribution of the children among a great many homes must have been a mammoth task for George Chapman, the appointed billeting officer, who held the post of the UDC's rates and housing administrator. Suddenly finding themselves in a totally unfamiliar place amongst strange people, not all evacuees were happy at Wymondham – at least not at first. The country way of life was alien to theirs, but many – though not all – eventually became contentedly settled.

NORWICH ROAD, WYMONDHAM.

In September 1939 the Women's Institute Hall on Norwich Road, just seen on the immediate right of the picture, was being used as a collection point for clothing, books, toys and other items for the evacuated women and children. The WVS, who also organized a knitting guild to provide comforts for the troops, helped with the distribution. Later the hall was occupied by the military and at one time there were three tents and a field kitchen on the adjoining land. With the opening of the Central Hall in December 1965, the W.I. Hall became redundant and was demolished to make way for housing.

Gravesend evacuees in the brickyard at the Melton Road home of Bert and Rose Myhill, who looked after them "like their own". Molly Welfare is in the middle of the front row, while her sisters Peggy and Betty are behind, either side of a Wymondham girl called Joyce who is holding the doll. The other children were also evacuees.

The quadrangle of the Senior School at the time of its opening. From 11 September 1939 a shift system saw junior and senior pupils from Gravesend work afternoons, while Wymondham scholars took the morning session. On 9 October Gravesend's juniors were transferred to the Junior School at Browick Road and normal hours were resumed at the Senior School. Already at Browick Road, infant evacuee children were working in the 'old junior block across the playground in the charge of two teachers and one keeper from Gravesend Gordon School'.

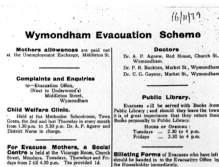

16/11/39

Wymondham Evacuation Scheme

Mothers allowances are paid out at the Unemployment Exchange, Middleton St.

Complaints and Enquiries to—Evacuation Office, (Next to Underwood's) Middleton Street, Wymondham

Child Welfare Clinic.
Held at the Methodist Schoolroom, Town Green, the 2nd and last Thursday in every month from 1.30 p.m. to 3.30 p.m. Dr. A. P. Agnew and District Nurse in charge.

For Evacuee Mothers, a Social Centre is held at the Vicarage Room, Church Street, Mondays, Tuesdays, Thursdays and Fridays from 2 till 4.30 p.m. Tea provided 1d.

Parish Nurses
Nurse Bennett, 3, Avenue Road, Wymondham
Nurse Thurgill, Spinks Lane, Norwich Common, Wymondham. Telephone 197

Boot and Clothing for Evacuee Children Fund. Hon. Treasurer, Mr. L. J. Turner, Manager, Barclays' Bank, Ltd., Market Street. Boots and Shoes, etc. may be left at the Evacuation Office during hours.

Doctors
Dr. A. P. Agnew, Red House, Church St., Wymondham.
Dr. P. R. Buckton, Market St., Wymondham
Dr. C. G. Gaynor, Market St., Wymondham

Public Library.
Evacuees will be served with Books from Public Library ; and should they leave the town it is of great importance that they return their Books personally to Public Library.
Hours of Opening :
Tuesdays ... 2-30 to 4 p.m.
Fridays ... 2-30 to 4 p.m.

Billeting Forms of Evacuees who have left should be handed in to the Evacuation Office by the Householder immediately.

Ambulance.
Men over 35 are wanted for the various Ambulance Squads in connection with A.R.P. and Volunteers are asked to apply to Dr. P. R. Buckton, Commandant St. John's Ambulance Brigade.

GAS MASK CARRIERS obtainable at GEO. R. REEVE, Model Press, Wymondham
1s. each

A notice from November 1939 listing some facilities for evacuees. With the Phoney War giving perhaps a false sense of security, it was reported on 7 November 1939 that only 325 Gravesend evacuees remained, 66% having returned home. Of some 70 other evacuees received 59 had returned home. This trend continued for the next few months, but a hard core stayed.

Just before Christmas 1939 some parents of evacuated children travelled to Wymondham to see their offspring in their wartime homes. Taken in Wymondham Market Place with the International Stores in the background, parents and children are shown together just before the parents travelled back to London. Around the same time the Mayor and Mayoress of Gravesend also visited the evacuees and distributed presents.

With Best Wishes for a Happy Christmas from the Directors of The Briton Brush Co. Ltd. and their grateful thanks for your services on patrol duty.

Christmas 1939

A Christmas card issued in 1939 by the directors of the Briton Brush Company in Lady's Lane to their own fire-guards. Other concerns like the Co-operative Wholesale Society's brush factory and the railway station had their own fire-watching teams.

As these adverts show, townsfolk were determined to have a good Christmas in 1939. The Phoney War was still being played out – until April 1940 when the Nazis invaded Denmark and Norway.

19

1940-1941

26 May – 4 June 1940 – *successful evacuation of 338,226 allied troops from Dunkirk.*

22 June 1940 – *France capitulated.*

10 July – 31 October 1940 – *The Battle of Britain won by the R.A.F.*

22 June 1941 – *Germany invaded Russia.*

7 December 1941 – *Japanese attacked Pearl Harbour and America entered the war.*

By January 1940 there were only 190 evacuees left in Wymondham, but once the Phoney War ended and the London area became a regular target for German bombers many more arrived. By the beginning of September 1941 the evacuation committee reported that the number of evacuees in the town had risen to 965.

Audrey Hammond of Silfield sits in a pedal car, while Paul Bevis, a Gravesend evacuee, holds the rope which pulled it. Behind are Mrs Clarice Hammond and Mrs Amy Bevis, Paul's mother, holding her younger son David. The Bevis family were lodging in the Hammond home.

I WISH TO MARK, BY THIS PERSONAL MESSAGE, my appreciation of the service you have rendered to your Country in 1939.

In the early days of the War you opened your door to strangers who were in need of shelter, & offered to share your home with them.

I know that to this unselfish task you have sacrificed much of your own comfort, & that it could not have been achieved without the loyal co-operation of all in your household. By your sympathy you have earned the gratitude of those to whom you have shown hospitality, & by your readiness to serve you have helped the State in a work of great value —

Elizabeth R

Mrs. Hammond.

In May 1940 the Queen sent this message to Mrs Hammond and many other locals who had given refuge to evacuees.

20

A get-together to celebrate the golden wedding of John and Elizabeth Wharton on 7 July 1940. Wymondham's evacuee billeting officer George Chapman is second from the right in the back row, while in front of him is his wife Eva. Betty Hoiles, an evacuee, is next to the Chapman's son Philip and second from the left in the front row. Like other evacuee children the Chapman's accommodated, Betty became part of the family.

BRIDEWELL STREET, WYMONDHAM.

In October 1940 the old Manor House in Bridewell Street became an evacuee mothers' club, first having being cleared and furnished by the Women's Voluntary Service. The Urban District Council gradually requisitioned empty houses as they became vacant for evacuee families and by the end of the war it had acquired thirty such dwellings. Large evacuee families also used 'hostels' in Middleton Street and Damgate.

Discussing matters of mutual interest over a cup of tea and biscuits, evacuee mothers from the 'bombed London areas' are seen at their Manor House club, soon after it had been opened. Some mothers helped to run the establishment, which included a toddlers' playroom stocked with books and toys donated by townsfolk.

In December 1940 evacuee mothers and children enjoyed a Christmas party at the Senior (now High) School. Arrangements were made by the Women's Voluntary Service and during the war the parties became an annual event. Sir Raymond Boileau of Ketteringham Park provided Christmas trees and each child received a present.

Some of Wymondham's enthusiastic ARP wardens. Having been trained in such practices as rescue, dealing with gas attacks and extinguishing incendiary bombs, they were geared to any emergency. About twenty ARP posts and points were established around the parish, while in June 1940 the ARP gas van was stationed on the King's Head Meadow. Locals were conducted through the van to test their gas masks. Pictured in this First Aid Party are Back row (left to right): W.Tunaley, 'Dido' Mabbutt, W.A.Gosling. Front row: C.Robey, W.Cowles and H.Smith.

Charles Eric Standley ready in case of a gas attack. Mr Standley was in charge of the No.8 ARP depot, which was based at his Little Dustpan ironmonger's shop in Town Green. He is seen here in the yard at the rear.

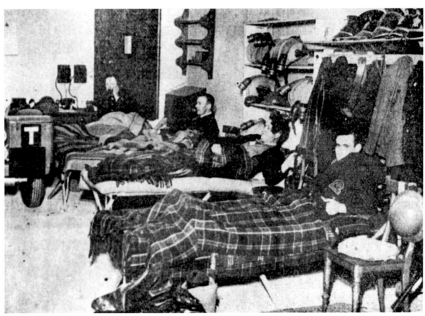

At the time this picture was taken in February 1940 two regular and four auxiliary firemen slept at the fire station in Market Street every night. The night shift was undertaken voluntarily and was much appreciated by the townspeople. Since the outbreak of hostilities the brigade's strength had been increased by the addition of about 30 auxiliary firemen "under the ARP scheme".

The fire brigade had sub-stations at Joe Smith's garage in White Horse Street, seen here in the left foreground, and at the old Drill Hall in Drill Yard alley off Cock Street. Each sub-station housed an older type vehicle which carried equipment, including a light pump and ladders.

The Wymondham Auxiliary Fire Service in early June 1940. With the existing ranks expected to be considerably thinned by military call-ups, there was an urgent appeal for recruits aged over forty. Among those pictured are Reg Cullum (first left kneeling) and Rev.J.Holmes (first right standing), a curate at the Abbey Church and for a time AFS commandant. In September 1941 the Auxiliary Fire Brigade was transferred to the National Fire Service.

The Briton Brush Company factory was used almost entirely for the duration of the war in the production of brushes and other items for the military. Products ranged from shaving brushes to road sweepers for airfields. Well over 100 male employees joined the forces causing a shortfall of labour. However, ladies who were eligible for some form of national service could count a job at the factory as work of national importance and did not have to be directed to other vital employment or the armed forces.

Briton Brush Company fire-watchers A.J. 'Bunty' Long (left) and George Mabbutt in the Spring of 1941. The fire-watching team was manned on a rotational basis and sometimes duties had to be worked in with other civil defence commitments.

In April 1940 Attleborough's famous Gerry Lee Band played for the local police dance in aid of the Norfolk Constabulary Widows and Orphans Benevolent Fund. The successful dance could not be held at its traditional venue, the Wymondham W.I. Hall, which had been requisitioned by the military, so it was switched to the Works Hall of the Gaymer's Cider factory at Attleborough.

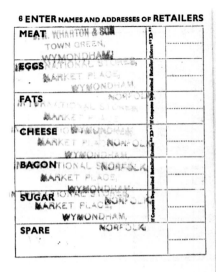

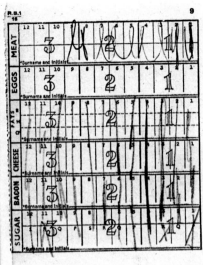

To ensure supplies were shared equally food rationing began on 8 January 1940. At first bacon, butter, ham and sugar were rationed, but it was soon extended to all basic foodstuffs. Families were issued with ration books to enable them to obtain their weekly quotas. Clothes rationing began in June 1941 and the popular slogan was "Make Do and Mend". Coal was rationed from 4 July 1941.

In response to the national 'Dig for Victory' campaign, the Wymondham Horticultural Association was founded in May 1940. Garden and allotment holders were urged at a meeting to contribute to the national war effort by keeping at least their own families in vegetables. In August 1940 a disposal depot for surplus fruit and vegetables was established at the Market Street premises of J.R.Wharton & Sons, butchers.

Members of the Spooner Row Women's Institute in the first week of September 1940 when they made 3,551 pounds of jam. The jam was sold to raise money to buy Christmas comforts for the troops. Any surplus jam was stored at Wattlefield Hall, the home of Mrs Ruth Clarke, the W.I.'s president (second from the right at the back).

Further funds were raised by schoolchildren collecting rose hips and taking them to the Market Cross where they were sold to Savory & Moore of Tottenham for manufacturing purposes.

One of the posters issued to help the national recruitment of land-girls, which had begun in 1939. In April 1940 a recruiting campaign began in earnest in Norfolk, a traditional farming community.

28

A land-girl joins men in harvesting at Browick Hall farm. Duties for land-girls could include caring for animals, milking, bottling, milk delivery, harvesting, hay-making, hedging and weeding. Some drove tractors and became mechanics. At one point their minimum wage was 30/- (£1.50) for a 48 hour week with an overtime rate of 10d (4p) an hour. After paying for board and lodging they were left with 14/- (70p).

A party for the 457th Searchlight Battery of the 69th Searchlight Regiment at Cavick House in 1940. There were two searchlight batteries in the town, the other being at Browick. Later the 457th Battery moved to Brundall and the 456th came to Cavick. The group headquarters were at Cavick House.

Private Laurence 'Loll' Hofgartner (extreme right) of the Royal Fusiliers poses with colleagues outside Cavick House in 1940. Large numbers of troops continued to be stationed in the district and were invariably entertained, particularly at Christmas, in local homes. In January 1940 the Town Green canteen staff organized a dance and appealed for lots of ladies to turn up to partner the forces personnel.

Alf Harvey, Wymondham's legendary fish and chip man, seen outside the Green Dragon Inn in 1941 with, it is believed, members of the Herefordshire Regiment who were stationed in the area. Alf had joined the Royal Artillery in September 1940, but to his dismay was discharged on medical grounds five months later. Gertie, Alf's wife, is also in the picture.

The new post office in Middleton Street was declared open on 29 May 1940 by Harry Clarke, then chairman of the Urban District Council. Mr Clarke (second right) receives the key to unlock the door from Mr.J.R.Finch, the postmaster. Exchanges of letters between loved ones, parted by war, were a great morale-booster.

Throughout the war families anxiously waited for news of their menfolk serving abroad. The picture shows Wymondham men with the 257th Battalion of the Norfolk Yeomanry, Royal Artillery, in France on 13 May 1940. At the post, which is an air raid signal, is Archie Clarke, son of the landlord of the White Horse pub, and below him is Sergeant Cyril Ayton. At the time British troops were fighting a massive rearguard action and by 4 June 'Operation Dynamo' had seen 338,226 men rescued and back in this country. On 3 June Sergeant Ayton sent his family a telegram saying 'safe and sound in England', but Archie Clarke was to spend three years as a prisoner of war.

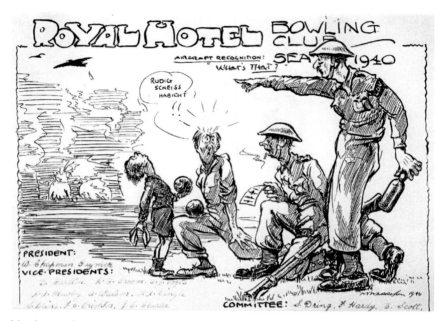

Members of Attleborough Royal Hotel Bowling Club making light of aircraft recognition at the heading of this list of officials and members for 1940. Although living in Wymondham my father George Yaxley was a member of the club.

On 24 July 1940 at Winston Churchill's behest, the Local Defence Volunteers were renamed the Home Guard and Wymondham became the headquarters of the 9th Battalion, which included companies from Attleborough, Cringleford, Hingham and Lopham as well as the town itself. The Wymondham Company (No.5 Coy) included villages such as Deopham, Hethersett, Morley and Wicklewood. The picture shows members of the Wymondham district Home Guard who were concerned with transport duties. The group included at least two bus drivers, one of whom was Mr Spinks (fourth from left in the back row).

Philip Fryer, Commanding Officer of the Wymondham Platoon of the Home Guard, 'on parade' with his children in the doorway of Browick Hall in March 1941. His son Richard with the hay, together with the basket of eggs, perhaps emphasizes the importance of food production during the war.

WYMONDHAM PLATOON, HOME GUARD.

On Monday, April 21st, this Platoon will be inspected by Field Marshal Lord Ironside, G.C.B., C.M.G., D.S.O.

All arrangements so far made for the ordinary Weekly Parades next week are therefore cancelled and in their place the following Rehearsals are substituted :—

TUESDAY, 15th April, 19.30 hours. Squads 1, 3, 7, 8, 11, 12.
WEDNESDAY 16th April, 19.30 hours.   Squads 4, 5a, 5b, 6, 9, 10, & Reserve.

Full details will be furnished at these Parades.   If you are unable to attend on your proper night as above, come to the other one.   Bring Rifle, and wear Belt and Anklets.

P. W. J. FRYER.

Drill Hall, Wymondham,
9th April, 1941.

Mr Fryer, who was often seen whizzing around on an old army motorbike, gave his men notice of an inspection in April 1941. The Home Guard used the Drill Hall in Pople Street, while the west tower of the Abbey Church served as a watch-tower with men undertaking four hours on and two hours off through the night.

Bert Caley sporting his Home Guard uniform outside his Northfield Gardens home. Bert was chief projectionist at the town's Regal Cinema, but in 1942 he would become the manager – and a legend in local cinematic history. During hostilities various war charities benefited from a percentage of the takings and collections held in the Regal. Perhaps because of increasing military call-ups, the numbers of the town's Home Guard were described in October 1941 as 'deplorably low' and efforts were made to remedy the situation.

Significant to defence pillboxes were built at strategic points, for example to guard major highways. Shown here are surviving examples at Cavick (left) and Spooner Row. These hexagonal pillboxes are type 22 and could accommodate six men with five light machine-guns (LMGs) and one rifle.

The type 22 pillbox, which stood by Browick Crossing on the important Norwich-Cambridge railway line was photographed by an American serviceman in 1943. At the time the picture was taken the road was that between the town and the bomber base at Hethel. Further out at Browick the surviving circular pillbox could have accommodated four men with three LMGs or rifles.

A surviving spigot mortar anti-tank gun emplacement on the London Road near Preston Avenue. Spigot mortar bases were small concrete cylinders with metal spikes designed for a 29mm spigot mortar (or Blacker Bombard as it was called). Among others was one situated at the front of Cavick House with the gun trained on the Tiffey Bridge at Becketswell.

There must have been great excitement in the area when news got around that on 22 February 1941 this German Heinkel plane had been brought down by anti-aircraft fire on a farm near Watton. The plane had been flying too low to allow the crew to bale out and two members were injured. The pilot officer, sporting an iron cross, and four crew were taken into custody at the local police station.

There were many events in the town supporting the Wymondham, Forehoe and Henstead War Weapons Week in April 1941. The town's target was £50,000 to purchase two bombers and two fighter aircraft, but in the event £132,081 was raised. A Spitfire fund, under the chairmanship of George Marwood, in October 1940 and a War Charities Week in late May and early June 1941 were just two of many successful fund-raising projects supported by the townsfolk.

The parade of troops and civil defence services personnel on the Market Place during War Weapons Week in April 1941.

Field Marshall Lord Ironside of Hingham, President of War Weapons week, inspects the parade on the Market Place. The firemen being inspected are from the right Arthur Banham senior, Herbert Ringer, Ben Dove and George Ayers. On the left is Reggie Bird, the brigade's Officer-in-Charge.

STIRRUP PUMPS.

FIRE PREVENTION — FREE ISSUE

NO.	ISSUED. DATE.	NAME & ADDRESS.
1.	20/10/42.	Mr.G.W.Yaxley, Bowden Terrace,London Rd.Wymondham.
2.	3/10/42.	Rev.C.Linnell, Vicar Street, Wymondham.
3.	20/10/42.	Mr. E. Mann, Chapel Lane, Wymondham.
4.	20/10/42.	Mr.E.W. Newton, Bellrope Lane, Wymondham.
5.	13/11/42.	Mr. J. Burt, Norwich Road, Wymondham.
6.	13/10/42.	Mr. J. Bowden, Norwich Road, Wymondham.
7.	20/10/42.	Mr. D. N. Guy, Fairland Street, Wymondham.
8.	10/5/43.	Mr. E.A. Hadingham, Bridewell Street,Wymondham.
9.	7/4/41.	Mr. Hammond.
10.	8/4/41.	Mr. Bull, Preston Avenue, Wymondham.
11.	12/5/41.	Mr. Duffield.
12.	7/11/43.	Mr. Percival. The Lizard, Wymondham.

With the end of the Phoney War civil defence activity increased and during 1940 Wymondham experienced 584 air raid warnings. The following year there were 671. Gradually stirrup pumps were issued and by February 1941 there was one for every twelve houses. Shown on this extract of a list, published later, are the names of some of the holders. In mid-January 1941 bins of sand were placed in various parts of the town for the use of householders should incendiary bombs be dropped.

A rescue party and the fire brigade from Wymondham assisted local services when high explosive and incendiary bombs were dropped by a single Nazi plane on the Gaymer's cider factory at Attleborough at 10.46 am on 30 December 1940. Shown is the damage inflicted in the factory's bottling department. Seven workers were injured, five serious, but nobody was killed. After dropping the bombs, the raider circled the town with its machine guns blazing, but there were no further casualties.

At 10.25 am on Sunday 2 February 1941 ten small high explosive bombs were dropped on the Lizard by a lone raider, who was probably aiming for the railway line. One bomb dropped on the road, shown here, outside the fourth house in from the railway and another behind that house, which was occupied by the Brown family. Twelve houses suffered the likes of dislodged tiles and broken windows, while there was damage to electricity, gas and water services as well as one telephone line. Beryl Brown recalled their chickens being frightened and some being injured. Seven bombs fell in a nearby gravel pit while another damaged a culvert under the railway line. Earlier, at 1.00 am on 22 June 1940, twelve bombs had been dropped on the Norwich Road – Tuttles Lane area, eight houses suffering broken windows and three damaged ceilings. At 6.14 am on 8 November bombs were dropped near Cavick House and on 13 November several unexploded bombs fell at Dykebeck and some were never recovered, while three houses were damaged at Spooner Row on 18 November. A day later it was the turn of Silfield Street with St Helen's Church, the school and four houses being hit. At 6.15 am on 11 December high explosives fell in fields at Park Farm and Coll's Farm Silfield, while at 10.50 am on 6 January 1941 Norwich Road was again the target when house roofs were damaged by machine-gun fire. At George Chapman's home there was a direct hit on a pair of boots! After that at the Lizard other bombings took place through the remainder of 1941, some damage being done to Chestnut Farm at Wattlefield that September. But in all the incidents, unlike other places in Norfolk, and Norwich in particular, no loss of life occurred in Wymondham.

1942-1943

15 February 1942 – *Fall of Singapore to Japanese*

16 April 1942 – *Malta awarded George Cross for its brave stand against unrelenting attack.*

4 November 1942 – *German-Italian army defeated at El Alamein.*

2 February 1943 – *Remnants of the 6th German army surrendered to Russians at Stalingrad.*

8 September 1943 – *Italy surrendered to the allies.*

With funding for the production of planes, ships, tanks and munitions always urgently needed, events to raise money continued unabated throughout the war.

Opened by Vice-Admiral E.H.Taylor, M.P. for Southwold, the local Wymondham, Forehoe and Henstead District Warship Week, staged in February-March 1942, brought in £100,843, enabling the adoption of the Navy frigate Hyacinth.

Army mechanised units in Warship Week parade when the salute was taken by Vice-Admiral Taylor at the Market Cross. In the Autumn of 1942 £805 was raised in the town for War Charities Week and, as a result of the District's 'Tanks for Attack' campaign, two Churchill tanks were to bear the name 'Wymondham'. At Christmas the Infant School pupils were raising money for the Red Cross Prisoner of War Fund.

Members of the Royal Observer Corps, followed by the A.R.P. wardens, parading up Market Street in the Warship Week parade. Leading the way are Arthur Ogden, who is saluting, and Dick Young. The Wymondham R.O.C. branch was founded around 1934 and the first observer post was in Hewitt's Lane, roughly on the site of the present Robert Kett school. The post consisted of a dugout with sheets of corrugated iron as the roof. Operators were equipped with a field telephone and binoculars; and they were connected to headquarters in Norwich.

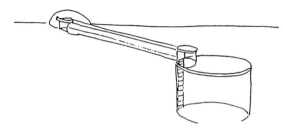

A diagram of a secret underground DF (Direction Finding) station which by 1942 was situated in a field off Tuttles Lane, opposite what is now Finderne Drive. It was housed in a cylindrical metal tank, not more than twelve feet in diameter, which was reached through a low doorway, then some ten feet along a gradually descending tunnel and finally about a further ten feet down a ladder. It housed wireless equipment attached to four surface aerials, together with a Morse Code Key and it was manned by Royal Signals personnel with a Sergeant in charge. The DF station was part of a network of such sites throughout the country and its primary purpose was to obtain a hearing on German signals, for example to keep an eye on enemy troop movements in certain areas. There was another site located in an adjoining field, but this was totally on the surface – 'a very ancient system'. The Tuttles Lane area was considered most suitable for the DF activity because of the flatness of the terrain with no high buildings or objects nearby to deflect radio signals.

In 1940 the home of the Semmence's transport at Norwich Road was requisitioned as a field bakery to supply local army units. The first bakery was manned by Royal Army Service Corps territorials who had escaped from France where they had been part of the British Expeditionary Force at St.Nazaire. On Whit Monday 1942 the 67th Mobile Field Bakery (RASC) arrived, taking over from the 18th Field Bakery. Two of the eight nissen huts used as barracks are shown at the top of the picture, taken later, while the large building housed the bread store.

Eric Barnicoat, from Cornwall, arrived with the 67th Field Bakery, who three months later were joined by the 70th. Some personnel had to be billeted off the site at the Abbey Schoolroom, the Queen's Head and the W.I. Hall. In August 1943 Eric married local girl Mary Barnard, a teacher who undertook pathfinding duties at a post on the Wreningham Road at Silfield. The reception at Underwood's tearooms in the town cost £4! In the Spring of 1944 both mobile bakeries moved out to the South of England to cater for troops destined to embark on D-Day.

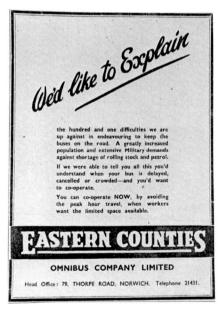

This Eastern Counties Omnibus Company's advertisement for June 1942 highlighted the difficulties of maintaining services in wartime. From time to time locals complained that they could not board buses because they were chock-a-block with service personnel. In the Spring of 1943 there was a problem with drivers parking their buses on the Market Hill. Edwin Gooch suggested charging them 2s 6d (13p), commenting, "That will stop it". But it did not happen.

Beatrice 'Beattie' Elvin (later Blake), pictured in her Women's Land Army uniform in April 1942, was employed at Browick Hall farm. Among her duties were delivering milk in a Ford van, while Audrey Townsend, a colleague, used a horse called Molly, and a cart for her deliveries.

INVASION

Each person, male or female, over the age of 16 years, living within the Wymondham U.D.C. Boundary is required to fill in and sign the form overleaf.

If you are already enrolled in any of the Civil Defence or Fire Fighting Services, or are already members of H.M. Forces, the Home Guard, the Royal Observer Corps or the Special Constabulary this must be stated.

You must realise that, when invasion takes place, all normal industrial, commercial and professional activities will for the time being cease, and every man and woman in the town, regardless of their normal work, will be required to assist in some capacity in overcoming and repelling the enemy.

On the instructions of the Norfolk County Council Emergency Committee with the approval of the Regional Commissioner and Military Commanders an Invasion Committee for this town has been formed. This is a voluntary committee and is composed of residents who have been charged with certain responsibilities in the event of invasion.

The duty of this committee is to see that everything possible is planned and arranged should invasion occur. It is working in your interests, and one of its main duties is to organise civilian parties and to ensure that every healthy person contributes in some way to the war effort in case of invasion.

Unless such detailed arrangements can be made NOW, and an adequate staff of helpers enrolled and trained NOW for the various jobs which will be required, nothing but confusion and disorganisation will result when the emergency occurs.

You are therefore required to fill in AT ONCE this form, sign it and add your address, and you will in due course be notified as to what your particular job will be.

E. G. GOOCH,
CHAIRMAN WYMONDHAM INVASION COMMITTEE.

This notice was issued in May 1942 by Edwin Gooch, chairman of the Emergency Invasion Committee, and shows it was still feared that the Germans might land. To counter any possible attack, the committee drew up a defence scheme involving the billeting officer, the Home Guard, the Civil Defence services, the Rest Centre (at Browick Road), the Fire Brigade and the police. Mr Gooch had taken over from Harry Clarke as chairman of the Urban District Council and the committee had been set up the previous year. Under the defence scheme the committee's civil headquarters were in the Council offices, while the new Drill Hall in Pople Street would serve the military and the Home Guard.

People of Wymondham !

WE are in the FOURTH Year of War.

A Wicked and Ruthless Enemy seeks to Destroy this Country.

The Peoples of the Occupied Countries— People like You, who lived in Towns like Yours—are Paying a Terrible Price because they were UNPREPARED FOR INVASION.

ANTI-INVASION Measures are intended to Protect the People.

BUT EVERYONE Must Know what to do if INVASION Comes.

It will be TOO LATE to Learn once the Enemy has Landed.

Those who could have Instructed you will be otherwise employed.

IT IS YOUR DUTY to Learn all you can about Anti-Invasion Measures NOW !

On September 20th
An *INVASION EXERCISE*
will be held in Wymondham.

This will be a rehearsal of what to do if the enemy lands.

Everyone MUST CO-OPERATE to the best of their ability so that the exercise will be a success.

We hope you will CO-OPERATE CHEER-FULLY.

To test the scheme would 'meet the conditions of imminent attack', a large-scale invasion exercise, code-named 'Harvest', was staged around Wymondham on 19 and 20 September 1942. Regular soldiers were given the role of the enemy and, during the 'action', Wymondham was reported 'bombed', some inhabitants 'rendered homeless', the Drill Hall 'blown-up' and the Briton Brush Company's factory 'burnt down'. The Norwich Mercury headlined its report of the proceedings: 'Exercise at Wymondham – Nazis captured a town in invasion exercise'. In spite of this, the exercise was considered worthwhile and many lessons were learned – not least that further First Aid Points should be established at the Methodist schoolroom in Spooner Row, Silfield Lodge, Harry Clarke's house 'The Chestnuts' in Cock Street and Seymour House on Norwich Road. The Priory in Middleton Street would be a Major Point with the mobile unit attached.

Pupils and teachers at Morley School in 1942. Behind them brown paper is stuck across windows to protect against splintering glass should a bomb burst in the vicinity. In early 1942 schoolchildren and youth club members in the area helped with collections in a waste paper drive. Over a ton of old books which once formed part of the town's library in the Market Cross were sent for salvage.

Wymondham firemen on parade for a training session at the Wymondham Laundry on Norwich Road in 1942. The Wymondham Fire Brigade would often rush to help in Norwich, particularly when the city was terribly blitzed in April of that year. When passing George Chapman's Norwich Road home on the way the engine's bell would be rung and again on the return journey. On the left of the picture is an Austin towing vehicle and on the right is the Dennis 'Ace' engine. Leading Fireman Reg Cullum, who was responsible for the training of 160 people attached to the brigade during the war then after became Station Officer, is on the extreme right, while Herbert Ringer, then in charge of the Wymondham control room, is on the left. About ten messenger boys under the age of fifteen years, including George Lister, Fred Hireson, Kenny Percival, Peter Wharton and Neville Whiting, assisted the Wymondham brigade. At the height of the Norwich blitz they had to carry messages between crews and keep in touch with the men on the hoses in case more pressure was needed.

There was horrendous devastation in Norwich following the raids of late April 1942. This was the scene some time after Curls large departmental store in Orford Place had been destroyed. In early May that year the Urban District Council sent a letter to the Mayor of Norwich expressing the sympathy of Wymondham folk on the loss of life and damage in the city "during the recent blitz". Later that month the City expressed thanks in the local press to all the helpers at Wymondham Rest Centre "for their untiring efforts towards those unfortunate citizens who had been rendered homeless after the recent raids".

The Baptist Church, which was quite severely damaged by incendiary bombs dropped from a single plane flying low on the early morning of Monday 27 July 1942. Incendiaries rained down on a number of houses and outbuildings in Brewery Lane, Friarscroft Lane, Fairland Street, Queen's Street and Damgate, as well as a warehouse on Chandler's Hill, causing roofs to catch fire. Bombs were also dropped on streets and fields, but the local fire brigade promptly dealt with the situation and there were no casualties. In June 1943 Harriet and Gilbert Clarke of Stalworthy Farm (also known as Dairy Farm), Suton Lane, forwarded the sum of £5:14s:2d (£5.71) to the Prisoner of War Fund. The money had been collected from people viewing a massive crater 70 feet deep with a 35 foot diameter made by a land-mine, dropped by parachute in one of their fields. When the crater filled with water it was used for swimming! At the same time another land-mine had fallen near The Sawyers pub in Sawyer's Lane, Suton. The intended target was probably the railway line. There were 106 air raid warnings in 1942 and 94 in 1943. Thereafter, they became less frequent.

Harry Tann, who lived at Anchor House on the Market Place and stands second from the right in the back row of these Wymondham A.R.P. wardens, used to recall the night when incendiaries fell on the Baptist Church. He had to climb up and throw them off the roof. This group of wardens became Southern Champions when Norfolk County ARP Services conducted a quiz competition in July 1943. Billy Clover stands on the extreme right.

In October 1942 the Urban District Council wrote to residents appealing for their cooperation in helping to provide 'home comforts' for American forces personnel who were beginning to arrive in the area. Pictured is an air crew at Hethel in mid-1943; and the opening of other United States 8th Army Air Force bases at nearby Deopham Green, Old Buckenham and Shipdham, as well as a hospital at Morley, ensured the Yanks would be a familiar sight on the town's streets until the summer of 1945.

B-24 Liberators from the 44th Bomb Group, based at Shipdham, over Wicklewood in October 1942. The workhouse can be seen below. Great numbers of American heavy bombers, Liberators and B-17 Flying Fortresses, became a very familiar sight in the sky as they headed out on a mission in the early morning and later returned home. But many never returned.

Wymondham Fire Service members William Howlett, Reggie Long and Barbara Long soon got to know their American allies at Hethel in 1943. November 1942 saw Americans at Hethel, but the first combat group, the 389th Bomb Group or Sky Scorpions as it was known, arrived there in June 1943. Almost immediately the group left for North Africa, from whence it took part in the famous strikes on the oilfields at Ploesti in Romania. It returned to Hethel in August 1943, remaining there until May 1945.

The first unit of medics to man the USAAF 77th Station hospital at Morley in October 1943. The hospital, built on the site of a golf course which had originally been requisitioned for agricultural purposes at the onset of hostilities, had been handed over to the Americans the previous month. About 700 workers had been drafted into the area to construct the buildings. In front is Sergeant Tommy Mann.

Wymondham girls with American friends at the Morley hospital. The girls are Joan Sheldrake (with guitar) and Peggy Oldfield. Every Sunday afternoon local girls would be picked up from the town and taken to the hospital to chat to patients. Mrs Pratt of the British Red Cross, who lived at Chapel Lane, organized the visits.

Looking down Market Street in 1943, the International Stores and Eastman's, the butchers, are on the near right. Over to the left with a sign swinging and a black car parked outside can just be seen the Mary Elizabeth Tearooms, a popular rendezvous for American servicemen, one of whom took this picture. Rationing presented problems and a food inspector would visit the café, an application having to be made for its allowance of basic items such as bread, meat, tea and sugar.

On a wet day two Americans cycle up Market Street, while locals stop for a chat. Perhaps the latest war news was being discussed. On the right can be seen the White Hart Inn with Herbert Ringer's fish shop and the 'On the Square Library Ltd' nearest the camera.

Damgate captured by an American. The bicycle was popular with the Yanks as a means of exploring the locality.

A water tank in the Market Place is clearly visible in this aerial shot taken from a Hethel plane in 1943. At the bottom right is Fairland Street and the top of Friarscroft Lane – an area hit by those incendiaries in that July 1942 raid. Another water tank in Town Green and the swimming baths in Brewery Lane were also kept topped up should fires start.

In July 1943 a 'monster gift auction' at the Wymondham saleground, off Fairland Street, raised about £1,700 for the Red Cross. Items of all descriptions from 'fat bullocks' to loads of gravel were donated for auction. It was said many of the gifts would prove useful 'to householders and farmers'.

The many events organized for Wymondham's 1943 War Charities Week included a 'United Nations Sports', a Grand Variety Concert and a boxing tournament which featured 'some very' attractive boxers who have fought in the Golden Gloves tournaments at Los Angeles, Chicago and Oklahoma City. Townsfolk broke their original target of £500 to raise £1,274. Other fund-raisers in the same year included 'Wings for Victory' week, 'Salute the Soldier' week and a 'Tanks for Action' campaign.

Banyard's Hall at Bunwell became a depot for a fleet of Church Army Canteen vans that were soon a common sight around the district. The vans served all allied units in South Norfolk and as far into Suffolk as the Indian Army personnel based at Elveden Hall, the R.A.F. at Shepherd's Grove and the Americans at Eye airfield. At the time Banyard's Hall was the home of Mrs E.K.Buchanan, who is in the middle of the front row. Mr Henry Buchanan is on the extreme right of the back row.

At Christmas 1943 American Army Air Force members distributed sweets, biscuits and other goodies to the town's children as they filed past the open front of Alf Harvey's fish and chip shop in Damgate. Military police controlled the traffic and the long queue of youngsters in the 'candy parade'. Children living in the outlying parts of the parish and those from some of the villages were given a great time at a nearby air base. The generous Yanks also held a party at the Senior School for over 300 scholars from the Browick Road Infant and Junior Schools. The pupils were addressed by Father Gerald Beck, chaplain to the Catholic group at the Hethel base.

1944

4 June 1944 – *Rome liberated.*

6 June 1944 – **D-Day** – *Allies landed in Normandy.*

13 June 1944 – *Flying-bomb (V.1) attack on Britain started. The first rocket bomb (V.2) fell on 9 September.*

25 August 1944 – *Paris liberated.*

17 September 1944 – *Black-out ends in most parts of Britain.*

The year 1944 saw Hitler's Third Reich take incessant poundings from both the U.S. 8th Army Air Force and the R.A.F. Many Americans flew from bases near Wymondham. After D-Day the American 231st Station Hospital at Morley became extra busy.

The control tower at Hethel in 1944. By 19 May that year, the Hethel-based 389th Bomb Group had flown 100 missions and on D-Day it flew a record four missions and two the following day.

The 389th Bomb Group's first assembly ship was named the Green Dragon after the popular Wymondham haunt of the Yanks from Hethel. Painted in bold green and yellow stripes, the Green Dragon was a war-weary B-24D Liberator, which crash landed at Manston airfield after an operation in July 1944. The pub sign had been adopted by Private Quakenbusch for use as the 389th Bomb Group's insignia.

Local girls pose with some of the men who ran the Hethel camp's store. Like other U.S. bases, Hethel was fairly self-contained, boasting among its facilities a chapel, a library, a gymnasium and a movie theatre.

From December 1943 to May 1945 Old Buckenham airfield was home to the 453rd Bomb Group. The group flew 259 missions in their B-24 Liberators with the loss of 58 planes and 366 aircrew. Hollywood legend James Stewart was Executive Officer at 'Old Buck' from March to July 1944, while Walter Matthau, later to find fame in the movies, also served there.

The Yanks enjoyed making a fuss of British kids and gave them goodies like candy, chewing-gum and comics. Pictured at Old Buckenham with their American friends are (left to right): Jo Jessup, Pauline Hardy and Joy Rix.

The 231st Station Hospital moved to Morley in March 1944 and for the remainder of the war served fifteen heavy bomber bases, a fighter group, support services and, after D-Day, American soldiers wounded in the battle to free occupied Europe. Under the command of the formidable Colonel Linwood M.Gable, a World War I veteran, the hospital's slogan was: "The patient comes first".

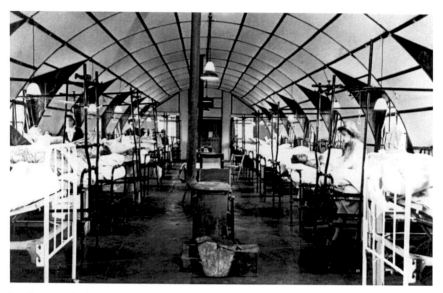

Inside a ward of the USAAF hospital at Morley many patients were recovering from horrific injuries and burns received on missions. But in the orthopaedic ward some patients were even receiving treatment as a result of 'Hitler's secret weapon' – the ordinary bicycle on which they had come to grief in Norfolk country lanes! One airman returned safely from an eventful trip to Berlin only to break his leg playing football the same evening.

Local girls with their American partners at a dance at the Deopham Green base, home to the 452nd Bomb Group from February 1944 to August 1945. With their B-17 Flying Fortresses the group flew 250 missions from the airfield, losing 158 aircraft (110 in action). The casualty rate in the spring of 1944 was exceptionally high.

A ground crew poses in front of The Little Gramper Junior. After returning home from a mission to Hamm on 22 April 1944 it crash-landed at Hethel. Two men were killed when it smashed into a radio shack (signals hut), but the crew were safe. Crashes were frequent and some accidental. On 8 February 1944 a B-17 of the 452nd Bomb Group crashed after take-off in Morley St.Peter 200 yards from Morley Hall, the eleven crew members being killed. Wymondham firemen attended and Fred Harwood of the brigade was slightly injured, while Fred Smith sustained more serious injuries when the plane blew up and was rushed to hospital. The Wymondham Fire Brigade attended a number of such incidents.

The Anglo-American Services' Club in Town Green, Wymondham, was situated in the old Picture House, which had closed in 1940. The club was officially opened by Colonel Lord Walsingham in March 1944. It was run by the Church Army under the auspices of the Ministry of Information and in charge was Captain Brown, whose helpers included volunteers from the local community.

British and American servicemen making friends in a corner of the Wymondham Anglo-U.S. Services' Club. The facility boasted a canteen, recreation room and dance area. To make the Yanks feel at home there were some dishes strange to England and innovations like a 'shoe-shine parlour'.

Attleborough had an Anglo-American Services' Club, situated in Station Road where the Connaught Hall now stands. This photograph was taken by Milton Edelman of the 453rd Bomb Group.

A dance in progress in the Attleborough Anglo-Services' Club. In the foreground local girl Norah Smith is partnering a serviceman.

Members of the 1986 Squadron of the Air Training Corps on a visit to the American base at Snetterton Heath in 1944. It was Len Manning, an evacuee who had been in the A.T.C. in London, who helped to form the squadron in 1941. The cadets, who had to be aged over fifteen and a half and under eighteen, came from Wymondham, Hingham, Attleborough and the district, the first Commanding Officer being William Purchase, headmaster of the Senior School where they met two evenings a week. Visits to American and R.A.F. bases were made and subsequently many cadets went on to serve in the air force with distinction. Mr.P.Bradstreet is second from left and Albert Humphrey fifth from left.

Wymondham's public houses were popular with American servicemen, who had nothing quite like them in the States. One picture was taken outside the Windmill pub on Norwich Road, while the other was taken in a room at the Woolpack, now Myhill's shop in Fairland Street. The Yanks enjoyed traditional pub games like darts and shove-halfpenny as well as singsongs round the piano.

Bicycles were hugely popular with the Americans as a means of enjoying the surrounding countryside and visiting neighbouring towns. Here an Old Buckenham G.I. poses outside the Three Boars inn at Spooner Row.

Market Street was snapped in 1944 by John Rex, a military policeman attached to the USAAF hospital at Morley. On the near left is the Men's Club, which opened its facilities to troops stationed in the neighbourhood.

An American serviceman stands on top of a heap of sand, no doubt placed by the Market Cross in the event of a need to deal with incendiaries. The top of the old underground toilets can be seen to the right. The railings were still round the Cross, though in July 1942 the Urban District Council had been ordered by the Ministry of Works to make a schedule of iron railings in the town which might be needed for making munitions. However, in March 1944 the Council were informed that "light railings were not now to be removed and as heavy iron was only 5% of the total this would not be removed at any rate for the time being".

Lieutenant Clyde Colvin, an 'Old Buck' navigator, in front of Cornelius Ramm's mill at Carleton Rode.

Attleborough presented a calm appearance when these three R.A.F. lads were photographed walking along Church Street.

Female members of the National Fire Service in the garden of its local headquarters at Whitegates, Hethersett in May 1944. Leading Firewoman Joan Bunn (second from left) worked on food allowances and rations for firemen. It was the N.F.S. that organized a dance during War Charities Week in August.

In early May the Trustee Savings Bank was promoting 'Salute the Soldier Week', the slogan for which was 'Support the Foot Sloggers'. In February the bank's Wymondham branch had been opened in the former offices of the clerk to the magistrates in Fairland Street. At its opening the bank offered a bank book with 5s (25p) already deposited to all children born in the Wymondham district in that month.

The programme for War Charities Week featured many events, including a Wymondham v. Searchlights Regiment cricket match, a baby show, a fancy dress parade, a brains trust, a horticultural show and a swimming-cum-diving gala. Music for the Home Guard's Grand Dance was provided by a USAAF band. All week in the vestibule of the United Services canteen at Town Green there was a photographic exhibition of the work of the Church Army.

Alf Harvey played his barrel organ in the streets to raise money for War Charities Week. A collection at the Regal Cinema, together with all the proceeds from its Sunday performance, helped to swell the fund, as did a flag-day and a trail-of-pennies event. Nearly £1,400 was raised, easily beating the £1,000 target for the town.

Pictured on D-Day, Emily Green used this specially made cycle-cum-trailer to take her children to Browick Road School from their temporary home in a cottage opposite the Chapel Bell pub on the Crownthorpe Road. Having been bombed out of their Norwich home in April 1942, the Green family had previously stayed on Norwich Road and then with cousin Fred Bunn on Tuttles Lane prior to moving to Chapel Bell. With his sisters Joyce and June, Ron Green is seen holding Flossy the dog. As late as July 1944 another 26 evacuees, consisting of nine mothers with their children, arrived in the town from Walthamstow to escape 'doodle-bugs' (flying bombs).

Ward tents were erected at the American hospital at Morley to cope with the mass admissions expected after D-Day. From July to the end of 1944 eight hospital train-loads of casualties, totalling 2,099 patients, arrived at Wymondham railway station from whence they were swiftly conveyed in a convoy of ambulances to the hospital. In September members of the Urban District Council visited the hospital on a conducted tour and met some of the soldiers wounded in the European invasion.

Watching baseball in the American hospital grounds. On the far side of the pitch behind a high fence can be seen the tents of the prisoners of war camp. There were about 200 German prisoners, who were put to work mostly keeping the hospital clean and tidy.

Gunner Bob Lister of the Royal Artillery was one of the many captured at the fall of Singapore in February 1942 and set to work building the notorious Thailand-Burma railway. It was not until July 1944 that the Norwich Mercury was able to report that he was alive and a prisoner of war in Thailand. Many Wymondham folk waited a long while, sometimes years, for news of their loved ones abroad – and for many the news was heartbreaking.

Officers of the 2nd Combat Wing 8th USAAF at their Ketteringham Hall headquarters. Movie legend James Stewart moved from the Old Buckenham base in July 1944 to become the 2nd Combat Wing's Chief of Staff as a Lieutenant Colonel. He is second from left in the front row.

Many locals were among the staff of the American Red Cross club at Ketteringham Hall. The club included a canteen and a rest room with plenty of candy, food and drink on offer. Sometimes bands played there. Ronnie Middleton (first on the right) undertook duties which ranged from lighting the boilers to cleaning cups. Ronnie Thurston is in the middle of the back row with Connie Eaglen (later Farrow) second from left at the back. In the middle of the front row is 'Tommy', an R.A.F. batman seconded to the Americans. Mrs Middleton sold sweets and chocolate at the club's counter, but could not eat them!

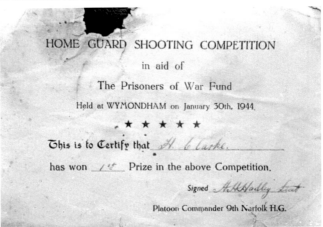

As this certificate shows, Horrie Clarke was one of the crack shots in the Wymondham Home Guard when a rifle shooting competition was held in January. In another contest for the 9th Norfolk Battalion held at the Garboldisham range in October the Wymondham Company took all the honours, one of its stars being Albert Stannard, who worked on Browick Farm run by Philip Fryer, the Wymondham Company's C.O. The Home Guard stood down in December 1944, being described at the time as 'a decisive deterrent to invasion'.

The Pulse Jet engine from a German V.1 flying-bomb, which came down on an elm tree at Browick Hall farm on 10 November. The "doodle-bug" or "buzz bomb", as such weapons were termed, was probably heading for the 389th Bomb Group base at Hethel airfield, but was put off course. The plane part of the device became separated from its pulse jet and blew up a little further on, taking out some windows of the hall.

The remains of a German V.1 flying-bomb which fell near the bomb dump of the USAAF's base at Deopham Green in late 1944. It did little damage, but caused plenty of excitement. From June 1944 V.1 flying-bombs and later V.2 rockets fell on the South-East, particularly London. Only a few came down in Norfolk.

Even though it was Christmas Day when these land-girls posed for the camera, cows still had to be fed and even milk had to be delivered. On the back row are (left to right): Laureen Chamberlain (later Ringer), Beatrice Blake (later Elvin), Irene Bartram (later Smith) and Mary Flatt. The front row is (left to right): Audrey Townsend, Doreen Wingrove and Freda Wicks.

Major Meyer Schindler, ear, nose and throat surgeon at the 231st Station Hospital of the American Army Air Force at Morley, playing Father Christmas to lucky local children. These pictures may have been taken at the Christmas party which Morley boy Derek Daniels remembered as taking place in the Red Cross clubhouse on 23 December. He commented: "They came and collected us from our homes in ambulances and took us back to the hospital where we had a great time".

1945-46

9 January 1945 – *Allies won the Battle of the Bulge.*

23 March 1945 – *British crossed the Rhine.*

7 May 1945 – *Germany surrendered (8 May V.E. Day).*

6 August 1945 – *First atomic bomb dropped on Hiroshima and 9 August second one dropped on Nagasaki.*

14 August 1945 – *Japan surrendered.*

8 June 1946 – *Victory Day celebrated.*

In the early months of 1945 the Allies continued to make progress and folk began to feel that the end of hostilities - at least in the European Theatre – could be in sight. However, some losses were still being sustained.

Returning from a mission to Magdeburg this B-24J Liberator of the 566th Bomb Squadron from Hethel crash landed at East Carleton on 16 January 1945. Running short of fuel, it narrowly missed a cottage, leaving a large part of its right wing in the garden.

The remains of a B-24 Liberator from the 453rd Bomb Group at Old Buckenham, which crashed and exploded at Crown Farm, Deopham, on 6 February 1945. The crash was caused by a mid-air collision on assembly resulting from propeller wash. Ten crew were killed.

Following a bombing mission to Aschaffenburg in January 1945 this B24L Liberator of Hethel's 564th Bomb Squadron crash landed at Fundenhall.

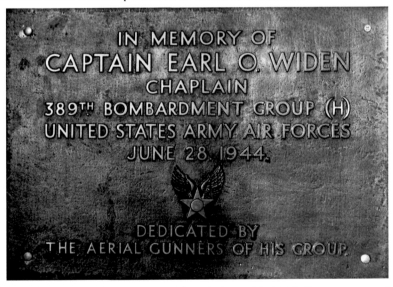

IN MEMORY OF
CAPTAIN EARL O. WIDEN
CHAPLAIN
389TH BOMBARDMENT GROUP (H)
UNITED STATES ARMY AIR FORCES
JUNE 28. 1944.

DEDICATED BY
THE AERIAL GUNNERS OF HIS GROUP.

In February 1945 the aerial gunners of Hethel's 389th Bomb Group presented this bronze plaque to the Congregational (now United Reform) Church in memory of Captain Earl Widen, a Protestant chaplain on the base, whose untimely death had occurred in 1944. With Rev.William Gayton, the minister, in poor health, Captain Widen was one of several U.S. chaplains who had helped out by taking services at the church. A similar plaque was received after the war from Chaplain Widen's home church, The Bethlehem Baptist church of Minneapolis.

On V.E.Day to celebrate Victory in Europe the Mary Elizabeth Tearooms in Market Street collected £4 for the town's Victory Fund, which then stood at almost £500. Wymondham was gaily decorated and the Market Cross floodlit after dark, while children's teas were organized and numerous bonfires lit.

During the two-day national holiday a thanksgiving service, organized by the Free Church Council, was held on 9 May 1945 at the Congregational Church. The previous day a similar service had been held at the Abbey Church. Amongst this group outside the Congregational Chapel is Chaplain L.W.Wickham, based at the American hospital at Morley, who sometimes preached at the chapel. On the extreme left is Peter Standley, who was awarded the D.S.C. for helping to sink a heavily armed trawler off the Dutch coast two years earlier.

U. S. Army Air Base

DEOPHAM GREEN

The Commanding Officer & Officers

request the pleasure of the company

of Miss Joan Welham

at a Dance

On Saturday, 19 MAY 1945

at 8 o'clock till 12 midnight.

R.S.V.P. to

LIGHT REFRESHMENTS

ADMISSION BY INVITATION ONLY

P.T.O.

The USAAF joined in the celebrations with dances held regularly on bases until the Americans departed for home. On V.E. Day evening a large crowd attended a dance at the Anglo-American Club in Town Green, while there was a party at the Morley hospital. The Gable Gators, the hospital's own band named after the C.O. Colonel Linwood M.Gable, was playing at the famous Red Cross Club at Rainbow Corner on Shaftesbury Avenue, London, when news of the cessation of hostilities in Europe reached the capital.

With the leaders of the 'Big Three' wartime Allies – Roosevelt, Churchill and Stalin – depicted, Armstrong's house furnishing shop in Attleborough High Street is decorated for the celebrations. An American serviceman stands in the doorway. President Franklin D.Roosevelt had actually died in April with victory in sight and had been replaced by Harry S.Truman.

Norfolk War Agricultural Executive Committee

DISCUSSION

MEETING

WYMONDHAM

SENIOR SCHOOL

FILMS for Milk Producers and Cowmen

Thursday, May 31st

At 7.30 p.m.

An advertisement for a meeting in May 1945 aimed at boosting milk production. As late as September 1949 the week's milk ration was limited to two and a half pints. With a world of food shortages, farming was to be just as crucial in the immediate postwar years as it was during the conflict. Three months before this advert appeared, the Wymondham Young Farmers' Club had been formed with Philip Fryer as chairman.

In early June 1945 Mrs Ethel Gooch presented prizes following 'the hoeing and singling competition for members of the Women's Land Army employed by the War Agricultural Committee in Norfolk'. The event took place at Stanninghall. As President of the Wymondham Women's Institute, the town's County Councillor since 1931 and local Women's Voluntary Services organizer, Mrs Gooch, Edwin's wife, was heavily involved in the community's war effort and described at the time as 'the embodiment of a good citizen'.

A General Election was held on 5 July 1945 – the first since 1935. A G.I. poses in front of a poster featuring Prime Minister Winston Churchill. The poster advertises a meeting at Wymondham Central School, Browick Road, in support of Colonel J Sandeman Allen, the Conservative candidate for South Norfolk. The election results were not announced until 26 July and in the South Norfolk constituency Major Chris Mayhew (Labour) secured a 5,963 majority over Colonel Allen. In a Labour landslide Wymondham's Edwin Gooch took the North Norfolk seat by a 5,246 majority over Sir Thomas Cook (Conservative).

In the summer of 1945 Edith Leverett (later Childerhouse), a Wymondham girl, received this card drawn by her American boyfriend. Previously he had been stationed at Hethel, but was then in Austria.

WYMONDHAM
WAR CHARITIES' WEEK

**SATURDAY, AUGUST 4th, to
SATURDAY, AUGUST 11th**

GRAND VICTORY
SHOW

Wymondham and District
Fur and Feather Society

**OPEN PEN SHOW SATURDAY,
AUGUST 11th, 1945, at SENIOR
SCHOOL, WYMONDHAM**

34 CLASSES FOR RABBITS
NUMEROUS SPECIALS

Schedules from E. Minns, Hon. Sec.,
2, Damgate Street, Wymondham.

RAIL STOCK WELCOME
ALL PROCEEDS TO ABOVE FUND

Other events include Dances, Cricket
Match, Sports, Horticultural Show,
Baby Show, Comic Dog Show, Brains
Trust, Keep Fit Display and many
other novelties.

With atomic bombs having just obliterated Hiroshima and Nagasaki, the fall of Japan must have been eagerly anticipated when the Wymondham and District Fur and Feather Society's 'Grand Victory Show' was held on Saturday 11 August 1945. When V.J. Day arrived on the 15th of the month it was celebrated with singing and dancing on the Market Place, while a huge bonfire was lit on the Fairland.

The War Charities Sports were held on the King's Head Meadow on the evening of V.J. Day. They had been postponed from August Bank Holiday Monday. A ladies football match was also played.

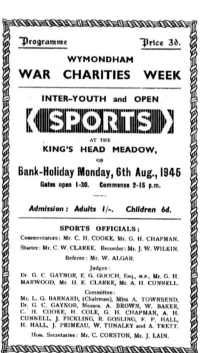

Programme   **Price 3d.**

WYMONDHAM
WAR CHARITIES WEEK

INTER-YOUTH and OPEN

SPORTS

AT THE
KING'S HEAD MEADOW,
ON
Bank-Holiday Monday, 6th Aug., 1945
Gates open 1-30.   Commence 2-15 p.m.

Admission : Adults 1/-.   Children 6d.

SPORTS OFFICIALS :
Commentators : Mr. C. H. COOKE, Mr. G. H. CHAPMAN.
Starter : Mr. C. W. CLARKE. Recorder : Mr. J. W. WILKIN.
Referee : Mr. W. ALGAR.
Judges :
Dr. G. C. GAYNOR, E. G. GOOCH, Esq., M.P., Mr. G. H.
MARWOOD, Mr. H. E. CLARKE, Mr. A. H. CUNNELL.
Committee :
Mr. L. G. BARNARD, (Chairman), Miss A. TOWNSEND,
Dr. G. C. GAYNOR, Messrs. A. BROWN, W. BAKER,
C. H. COOKE, H. COLE, G. H. CHAPMAN, A. H.
CUNNELL, J. FICKLING, R. GOSLING, F. P. HALL,
H. HALL, J. PRIMEAU, W. TUNALEY and A. TRETT.
Hon. Secretaries : Mr. C. CORSTON, Mr. J. LAIN.

H. G. STONE AND CO. (PRINTERS), LTD., WYMONDHAM AND ATTLEBOROUGH

In the days following the Japanese surrender various Victory tea parties were held in the town. On the Lizard Mr Percival, a shopkeeper and baker, entertained 54 children aged under 14 to a bun fight in his yard, which was decorated for the occasion. A good tea was followed by minerals and ices – and each child was given one shilling (5p) and a present. After tea sports were held for all ages, the prizes being presented by an Old Mother Riley look-alike. Like many children in Wymondham those at Norwich Common enjoyed a trip to Great Yarmouth – the first time some had seen the sea.

With the prospect of many men returning from the forces – some to get married – it was obvious that there would be an acute shortage of housing in Wymondham. In September 1945 Edwin Gooch, U.D.C.Chairman, performed what was claimed to be the first bricklaying ceremony in the county so far as permanent postwar council houses were concerned. It was the start of the erection of 16 council houses in Silfield – the first of many – to meet the demand. R.C. (Bob) Carter, the contractor, is on the left of the picture, while among councillors watching are Frank Clarke (next to Mr Carter), Harry Clarke (sporting a trilby), Ethel Gooch and James Underwood (extreme right). Tom Turner, who became a legendary town clerk after Lionel Standley retired from the post in October 1948, stands behind Frank Clarke.

The Anglo-American Services' Club closed in February 1946, having served more than 240,000 beverages in two years – at one period averaging 1,000 daily. Over 100 dances had been held there, as well as parties, social evenings, ENSA concerts, classical concerts and movie shows. In June 1945 the Wymondham Urban District Council had conveyed the good wishes of the townsfolk to the American forces in the locality on their imminent departure from England. In a few weeks they were all gone.

As the Americans left, Wymondham servicemen were beginning to return home and Wymondham railway station must have been a welcoming sight, particularly to those who had been prisoners of war. Among the many, Flight Sergeant Ivan Betts, a prisoner in Germany for over two years, arrived back in April 1945, while a month later saw the repatriation of Gunner Roy Godfrey of Suton, who had been a P-O-W since capture at Dunkirk in 1940.

The banner which welcomed home Captain Philip Hall, who had been a prisoner of the Japanese since the fall of Singapore in February 1942. Other ex-prisoners of war reaching home from the Far East, about the same time (late 1945) included Private E.J.Filby, Gunner Bob Lister, Sergeant Dennis Clarke, Sergeant Les Fields, J.Buttolph and Corporal C.Hawes. Some had served in the Norfolk Regiment.

REGAL CINEMA

Manager—B E. CALEY. PHONE 3140

PROGRAMME

Subject to alteration without notice.

Monday, June 3rd. **BOB HOPE** in (A) **The Princess and the Pirate** also DOGS AT WORK	Monday, June 17th. **Dana Andrews - Dick Haynes** in (U) **STATE FAIR** (Technicolour) also SUPPORTING PROGRAMME
Thursday, June 6th. **Dorothy Lamour - Eddie Bracken** in (U) **THE FLEETS IN** (RE-ISSUE) also SUPPORTING PROGRAMME	Thursday, June 20th. **NORMAN EVANS** in (U) **DEMOBBED** also (A) MIDNIGHT MAN HUNT
Monday, June 10th. Whit-Monday at 2, 5.30 and 8.15 p.m. **FLANAGAN and ALLEN** in (U) **Here Comes the Sun** also UNDER WESTERN SKIES	Monday, June 24th. **JOAN FONTAINE** in (A) **The Affairs of Susan** also SUPPORTING PROGRAMME.
Thursday, June 13th. **Basil Rathbone - Nigel Bruce** in (A) **Pursuit to Algiers** also (U) BABES ON SWING STREET	Thursday, June 27th. **SIR AUBREY SMITH** in (A) **Scotland Yard Investigator** also I'LL TELL THE WORLD

NOTE. To "A" Certificate Films, persons under 16 years will only be admitted accompanied by an Adult
SATURDAY AFTERNOON MATINEES. In the event of 'A' Certificate Programmes, Special Pictures will be shown.
Monday till Friday 7 p.m.   Doors open 6.45 p.m.   Bookings no extra.
Saturday—Matinee 2 p.m.   First House 5.30 p.m.   Second House 8.15 p.m.
Children Half-price Tuesday, Wednesday, and Friday Evenings.

The Regal Cinema's programme for June 1946 featured the movie 'Demobbed' – most appropriate for the time! In August 1946 as more men were returning home, local G.P. Doctor Agnew reported a high birth rate!

An invitation to a 'Welcome Home' dinner for men returning from the war. Two such dinners were held in May and October 1946; and were financed from a Victory Fund, which had been inaugurated in November 1944. Gaymer's cider factory at Attleborough provided free beer! The Victory Fund also assisted the British Legion in the provision of education and clothing for the children of prisoners of war. To commemorate victory it was decided to build a community hall, but it was not until 1965 that the Fund's balance was placed towards the Central Hall, which was then under construction. Likewise, the Welcome Home Fund at Spooner Row was earmarked for a social centre.

Eric Barnicoat (left) and next to him George Mabbutt enjoying life back in Civvy Street at the first British Legion dinner after the war. At a 'Welcome Home' social in Hethersett Colonel Sandeman Allen urged returning servicemen to join the Legion and the branches at Attleborough, Hethersett and Wymondham all saw membership increase.

The Wymondham Fire Brigade celebrate! On the left at the back can be seen the head of George Marwood, the leader of the Briton Brush Company's own fire section. During the hostilities the Wymondham brigade was alerted for 1,542 air raid warnings and attended over 30 aircraft crashes. For a time after the war the siren was used for calling out part-time firemen in the event of an incident. In 1948 the National Fire Service became denationalized and responsibility was delegated to County Councils. In September 1967 the brigade moved from the old fire station in Market Street to its present home on London Road.

Having being used as a reservoir in case of emergency the swimming pool was officially reopened in March 1946 by Councillor Frank Alpe, who gave three cups for competitions. Frequent users were the Norwich Penguins, but the picture shows R.A.F. personnel training in the baths after the war. Among other indications that things were getting back to some sort of normality in 1946 was the Town Football Club's 4-0 victory against Holt before over 1,000 spectators in the Wymondham Charity Cup. March also saw bananas on sale again in Norfolk!

To try and alleviate the housing shortage of an increasing population prefabricated temporary bungalows, colloquially known as 'prefabs', were introduced. By September 1946 fifteen of these dwellings had been erected at Park Lane, Wymondham, with the initial rent 10s 9d (54p) a week plus rates and water charges. Though originally envisaged as a ten-year stopgap, they lasted much longer and it is only in recent years that almost all have been demolished. The picture shows one boarded and ready for demolition.

Once the U.S. 8th Army Air Force left, the nissen huts at Ketteringham Park were taken over by squatters, one of whom is shown in the picture. In August 1946 the local press carried the story of a Mr.E.R.Seaborn, who moved his family into a nissen hut at Ketteringham Park a few hours before Forehoe and Henstead Rural District Council took over the site. Mr Seaborn, a Welshman who had served overseas with the Hampshire Regiment, was married to a Wymondham girl. The Hethel camp was also turned into a 'village' for hundreds of families waiting to be rehoused. The camp had its own shops, school and church, while there were even weekly film shows for the children and a cycle speedway track. It was as late as 1958 before the last families there were rehoused.

8th June, 1946

TO-DAY, AS WE CELEBRATE VICTORY, I send this personal message to you and all other boys and girls at school. For you have shared in the hardships and dangers of a total war and you have shared no less in the triumph of the Allied Nations.

I know you will always feel proud to belong to a country which was capable of such supreme effort; proud, too, of parents and elder brothers and sisters who by their courage, endurance and enterprise brought victory. May these qualities be yours as you grow up and join in the common effort to establish among the nations of the world unity and peace.

George R.I.

Saturday 8 June 1946 was designated Victory Day – and there were big celebrations in Wymondham and throughout the country. The day opened with the ringing of the Abbey Church bells and among numerous events were a sports meeting and a fancy dress parade. Each child in the town received a voucher for mineral water and ice cream, while the old folk, like their counterparts at Spooner Row, enjoyed a tea. In the evening the Market Place was floodlit and dancing to amplified music continued until midnight.

The Wymondham War Memorial lists the names of 43 servicemen from local families who were killed in World War II. Three civilians are listed as having died as a result of enemy action, but these deaths did not occur whilst the men were in the town.

George 'Spud' Middleton, who lived in White Horse Street, was among three people killed while working at Scottow Aerodrome (R.A.F.Coltishall) when high explosives were dropped by an enemy raider on 19 August 1940.

The 3rd Earl of Kimberley was killed on 17 April 1941 at 48 Jermyn Street, London, during a bombing raid when he was working at the War Office for MI5.

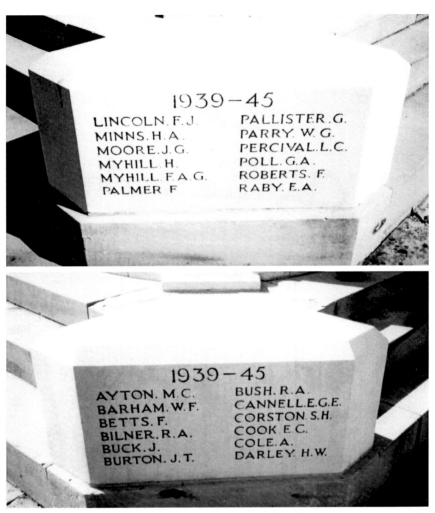

1939 – 45

LINCOLN. F. J.	PALLISTER .G.
MINNS. H. A.	PARRY. W. G.
MOORE. J. G.	PERCIVAL.L.C.
MYHILL. H.	POLL. G.A.
MYHILL. F. A. G.	ROBERTS. F.
PALMER F	RABY. E.A.

1939 – 45

AYTON. M. C.	BUSH. R. A.
BARHAM. W. F.	CANNELL.E.G.E.
BETTS. F.	CORSTON. S.H.
BILNER. R. A.	COOK. E. C.
BUCK. J.	COLE. A.
BURTON. J. T.	DARLEY. H. W.

John 'Jack' Mabbutt, who lived on Chandler's Hill and had been employed at the Co-operative Brush Factory, was killed on 25 July 1942 at Cartarton in Oxfordshire whilst working as an aircraft rigger at the Air Ministry Estate. He went up on a test flight (from R.A.F.Brize Norton) and the plane exploded.

The serious housing crisis was not the only huge problem that the Attlee government had to contend with in the immediate postwar years of extreme austerity. The winter of 1946-47, a terribly severe one, saw a serious shortage of coal and there were many power cuts. Basic foods such as cheese, milk, meat, tea and even bread were still rationed. Clothes were rationed until March 1949, but it would not be until 1954 that all rationing would end. The war had been won, but it would take longer to win the peace.

Appendix 1

Hit songs of the War

(The year in which they first became popular is shown in brackets)

Wish Me Luck As You Wave Me Goodbye (1939)
Over the rainbow (1939)
Hang out the Washing on the Siegfried Line (1939)
Run Rabbit Run (1939)

Kiss me goodnight Sergeant Major (1940)
A nightingale sang in Berkeley Square (1940)

The White Cliffs of Dover (1941)
Boogie-Woogie Bugle Boy (1941)

This is the Army, Mr Jones (1942)
We'll meet again (1942)
When the lights go on again all over the World (1942)
White Christmas (1942)

You'll never know (1943)
My heart and I (1943)
Lili Marlene (a much older German song, but it became popular with the Allies after Marlene Dietrich started to sing it in 1943)

I'll be seeing you (1944)
Mairzy Doats (1944)

Cruising down the river (1945)
My guy's come back (1945)
We'll gather lilacs in the spring (1945)

Appendix 2

Radio programmes of the War

Bandwagon (Arthur Askey, Richard 'Stinker' Murdoch)

The Brains Trust

Children's Hour

Forces' Favourites

Garrison Theatre (Jack Warner)

Hi Gang (Ben Lyon, Bebe Daniels)

ITMA (It's That Man Again, starring Tommy Handley)

Music While You Work

The Radio Doctor

Sandy Calling (Sandy Macpherson)

Sincerely Yours (Vera Lynn)

Variety Bandbox

Woman's Hour

Workers' Playtime

Wymondham entertains the military.

To
H.M. FORCES

This INFORMATION SHEET is issued by the Local Social Service (Entertainments) Committee to enable you to find Entertainment, Refreshment and Fellowship during your stay in this Town.

CANTEENS

1. The Social Service CANTEEN at rear of the Methodist Church, Town Green, is Open from 5 to 10 p.m., every day except Saturday and Sunday.
   Refreshments, Games, Table Tennis, Billiards, Snooker. Reading and Writing Room.   Papers and Magazines.
2. The Social Service CANTEEN at the Masonic Hall, Damgate Street, is Open every Saturday from 2.30 to 10 p.m., and every Sunday from 2.30 to 10 p.m.
   Refreshments, Games, Table Tennis. Papers & Magazines.
3. There is also a CANTEEN at Church Street, Open Daily from 5 to 10 p.m.

CLUBS

Open to All Members of H.M. Forces.
1. The Ex-Service Men's Club, (licensed), Queen Street.
2. The Men's Club, Market Street.
   By courtesy of the respective Committees.
Billiards, Snooker, and other Games available at both Clubs.

DANCES

For H.M. Forces and Friends will be held every Saturday at the New Schools, Norwich Road from 7.30 to 11 p.m. Admission 6d.
   As numbers must be strictly limited, Members of H.M. Forces will be admitted BY TICKET ONLY which may be purchased in advance at the Social Service Canteen.
   Ladies' Tickets will be sold at the Door only.
   All Men are kindly requested to wear Light Shoes or Plimsoles.
   Light Refreshments will be on Sale

LIBRARY

Books are available on loan free of charge at the Public Library, Becket's Hall, on Tuesdays and Fridays 2.30 to 4 p.m.

GEO. R. REEVE, THE MODEL PRESS

Appendix 3

Some highlights at the Wymondham Regal during the War years (actual date of film's release and names of main stars in brackets).

1939

Snow White and the Seven Dwarfs (Walt Disney, 1937)

The Adventures of Robin Hood (Errol Flynn, Olivia De Havilland, Basil Rathbone, 1938)

In Old Chicago (Tyrone Power, Alice Faye, Don Ameche, 1937)

1940

Destry Rides Again (James Stewart, Marlene Dietrich, 1939)

Wuthering Heights (Laurence Olivier, Merle Oberon, David Niven, 1939)

Road to Singapore (Bing Crosby, Bob Hope, Dorothy Lamour, 1940)

1941

All This and Heaven Too (Charles Boyer, Bette Davis, 1940)

The Ghost Train (Arthur Askey, Richard 'Stinker' Murdoch, 1941)

High Sierra (Humphrey Bogart, Ida Lupino, 1941)

1942

Foreign Correspondent (Joel McCrea, Laraine Day, George Sanders, 1940)

This Gun for Hire (Alan Ladd, Veronica Lake, 1942)

The Maltese Falcon (Humphrey Bogart, Mary Astor, 1941)

1943

Reap the Wild Wind (Ray Milland, John Wayne, Paulette Goddard, 1942)

Springtime in the Rockies (Betty Grable, John Payne, Carmen Miranda, 1942)

We Dive at Dawn (John Mills, Eric Portman, 1943)

1944

Five Graves to Cairo (Franchot Tone, Anne Baxter, Erich Von Stroheim, 1943)

Coney Island (Betty Grable, George Montgomery, Cesar Romero, 1943)

The Miracle of Morgan's Creek (Betty Hutton, Eddie Bracken, 1943)

1945

Going My Way (Bing Crosby, Barry Fitzgerald, 1944)

Double Indemnity (Fred MacMurray, Barbara Stanwyck, Edward G.Robinson, 1944)

Waterloo Road (John Mills, Stewart Granger, Joy Shelton, 1944)